THE NATURE KIDS GUIDE TO

MOUNTAIN LIONS

DAVID ANDERSON

LP Media Inc. Publishing
Text copyright © 2026 by LP Media Inc.

For information address LP Media Inc. Publishing,
30012 Variolite St NW, Princeton MN 55371
www.lpmedia.org

Publication Data

Mountain Lions
The Nature Kid's Guide to Mountain Lions — First edition.

Summary: "Learn all about Mountain Lions, the Nature Kid Way"
— Provided by publisher.

ISBN: 979-8-89818-124-6

[1. Mountain Lions – Non-Fiction] I. Title.

Title: The Nature Kid's Guide to Mountain Lions

CONTENTS

MOUNTAIN HOMES

Growl! A mountain lion stands on a rocky ledge. Its golden eyes scan below.

Mountain lions need wild places with room to roam. They live in forests, deserts, and swamps. But rocky mountains are a favorite home.

These big cats love areas with lots of cover. Tall grass and thick bushes help them hide. Trees give them shade on hot days. Rocky cliffs offer spots to rest and watch for **prey**.

Caves and dense plants shelter them from storms. Cold winters or warm summers do not stop them. They just need fresh water nearby to drink.

Each cat picks its own **territory** to call home.

COAST TO COAST

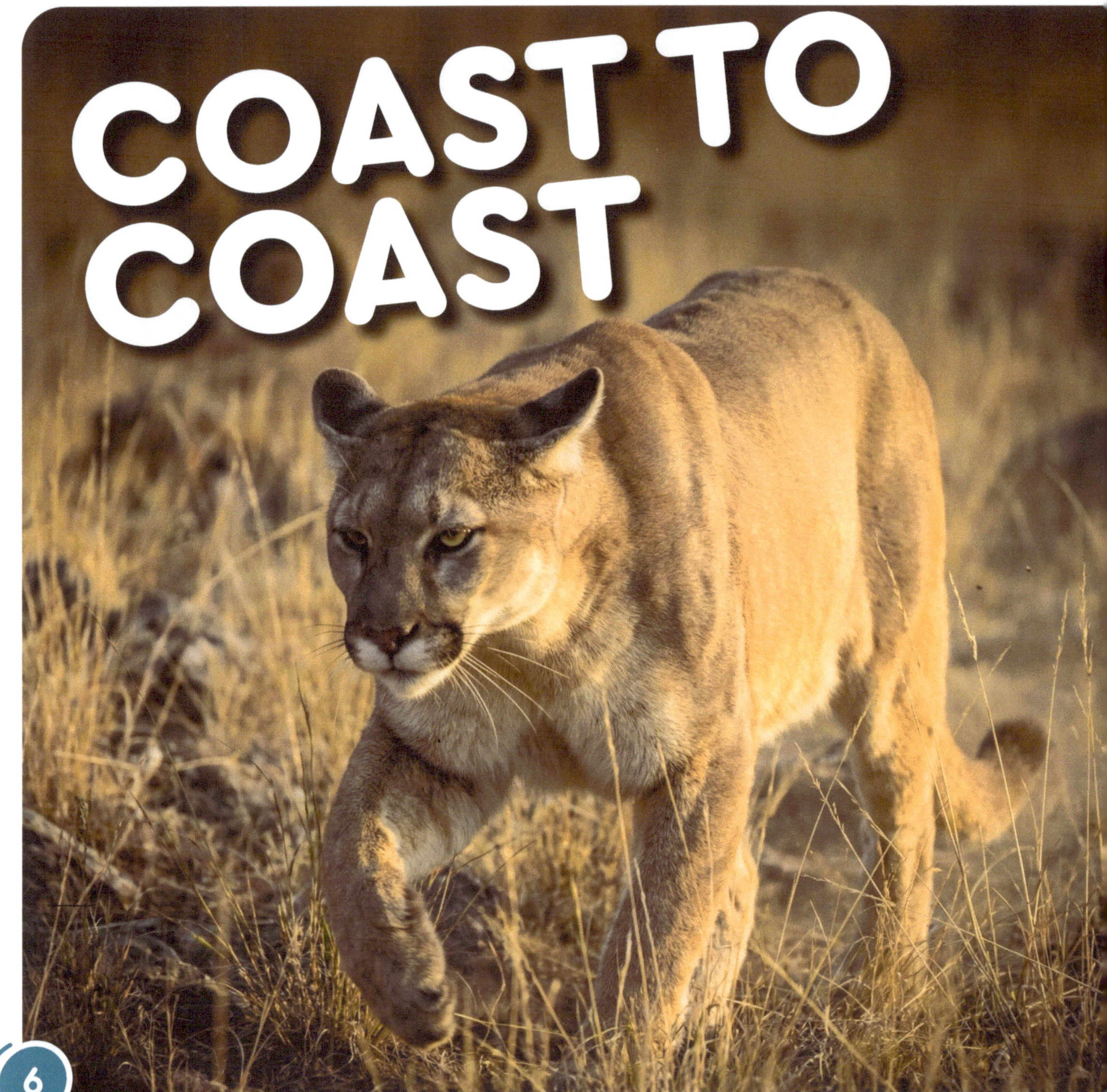

Swoosh! A mountain lion darts through tall grass. Its golden eyes scan.

Mountain lions only live in North and South America. They roam from Canada to Chile.

The Florida panther lives only in Florida. Western mountain lions live in California. They also live in Colorado.

In South America, pumas live in Argentina. They live in Brazil too. Andean pumas live high up. They live in the Andes Mountains.

Mountain lions can jump 18 feet straight up. That's higher than a giraffe is tall!

BIG CATS

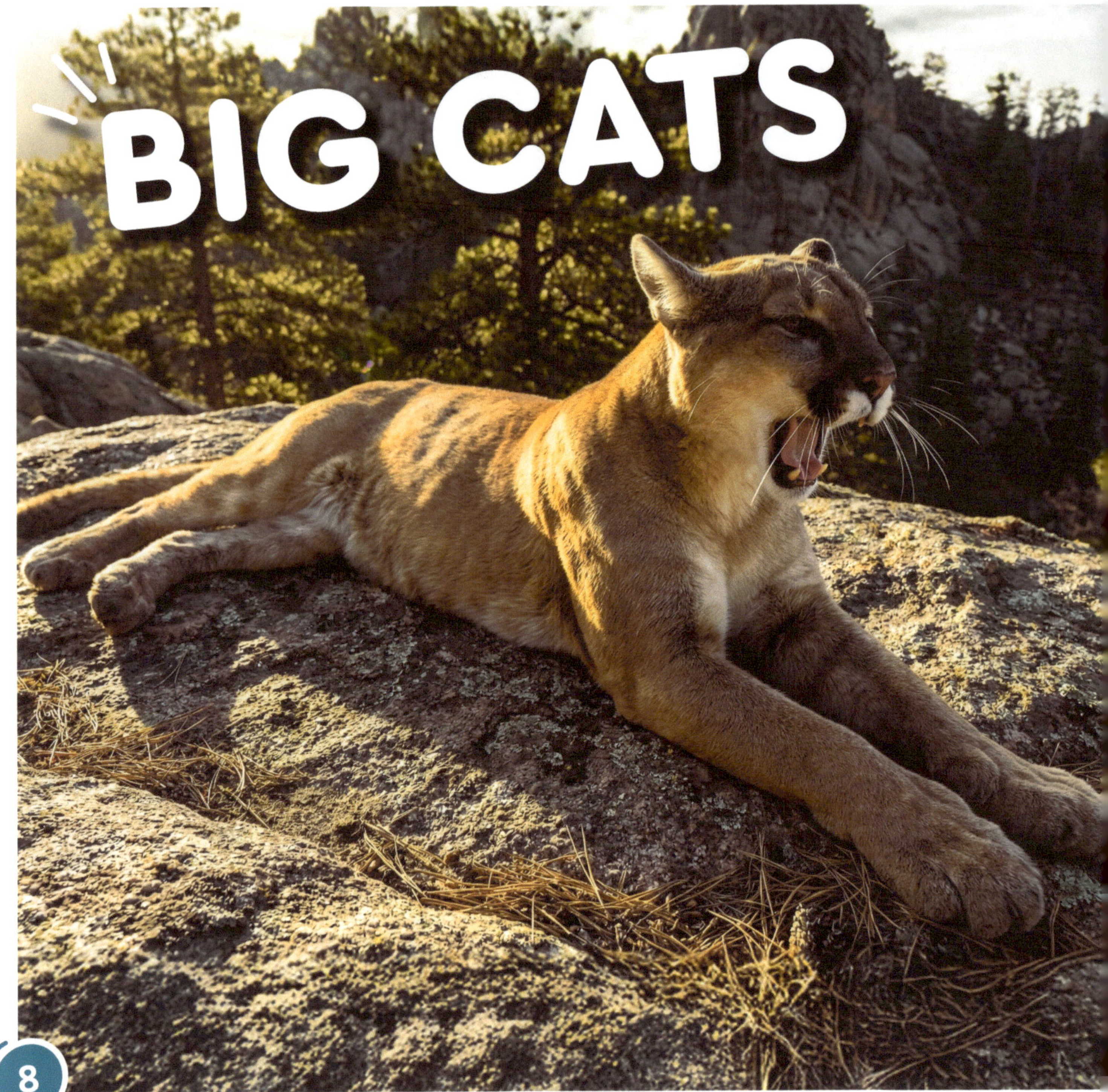

Yawn! A mountain lion stretches out on a warm rock.

Mountain lions cannot roar. So they are not true big cats. They are also not the biggest cats.

Lions and Tigers are larger. Jaguars also live in the Americas. They are bigger as well.

Male mountain lions are larger than females. A big male can be eight feet long from nose to tail. Males weigh between 120 and 220 pounds. Females are lighter, usually around 65 to 140 pounds.

Instead of roaring, mountain lions purr like house cats. They also chirp and scream!

BUILT TO HUNT
DID YOU KNOW?
Mountain lions can run 50 miles per hour. That makes them the fastest predator in the USA!

Shhhh! A mountain lion crouches low in the brush.

Mountain lions have bodies made for hunting. Strong back legs help them jump far. Sharp claws grip prey and help them climb.

Their front paws are wide and powerful. These paws pin down animals they catch. Thick pads on their feet make each step quiet.

Mountain lions have long tails that help them balance when they run and turn quickly.

Sharp teeth finish the job. Long fangs bite down hard. Their back teeth cut meat into pieces they can swallow.

SUPER
SENSES

Snap! A twig breaks at dusk. A mountain lion turns its ears.

Mountain lions have amazing senses. Their eyes see well in dim light. This helps them hunt at dawn and dusk.

Their ears can turn in different directions. Each ear moves on its own! This helps them find sounds in the forest.

They also have long whiskers. These help them move through tight spaces.

A mountain lion can hear sounds that humans cannot hear.

13

HIDDEN
HUNTER

Rustle! A mountain lion hides in dry leaves. It's fur blends in well.

Mountain lions are hard to see when they stay still. Their tan fur blends in with rocks and dirt. This helps them stay hidden from prey.

They also hide from danger. They often run away when a bigger moutain lion comes near. They avoid confrontation when they can.

Mountain lions are quiet too. Soft paw pads help them walk without making noise.

Mountain lions can leap 40 feet forward, that's longer than a school bus!

15

MEAT EATERS

Chomp! A mountain lion tears into fresh meat. It is hungry.

Mountain lions are **carnivores**. This means they eat meat. Deer are their favorite food. One deer can feed a mountain lion for many days.

They also eat smaller animals. Rabbits, squirrels, and birds are common meals. Sometimes they catch raccoons or porcupines too.

Mountain lions only eat meat. Their stomachs cannot digest leaves or berries. They get all their energy from meat.

DID YOU KNOW?

A mountain lion eats about ten pounds of meat a day.

SNEAK ATTACK
FUN FACT!
Mountain lions catch their prey only about one out of every four tries!
18

Hush! A mountain lion crouches behind a bush. It waits.

Mountain lions are ambush hunters. They do not chase prey for long distances. Instead, they sneak up close before attacking.

They move slowly and stay low to the ground. Their bodies press against rocks or grass. They wait for the right moment to strike.

When prey is close enough, they leap! Their strong back legs push them many feet through the air. They land right on top of their prey.

A quick bite to the neck ends the hunt. This all happens in just a few seconds.

WATCH OUT

Hiss! A mountain lion bares its teeth. Back away slowly!

Mountain lions are **apex predators**. They have no natural enemies that hunt them. This puts them at the top of the food chain.

Mountain lions usually avoid humans. They are shy and prefer to stay hidden. But they can still be dangerous.

If you see one, do not run. Running can make it chase you. Stand tall and make loud noises. Wave your arms to look big.

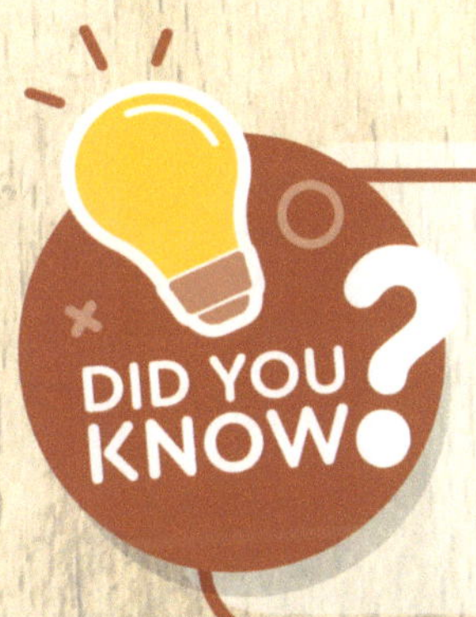

Mountain lion attacks are rare. Only four to six happen each year.

FAST GETAWAY

Whoosh! A mountain lion leaps froma rock and disappears in seconds.

Mountain lions are quick runners. They can reach speeds up to 50 miles per hour. But they can only run this fast for short bursts.

Speed helps them escape danger. If a bear gets too close, they run. Bears don't hunt them, but they are still scared of bears.

Mountain lions are better at quick sprints than long runs.

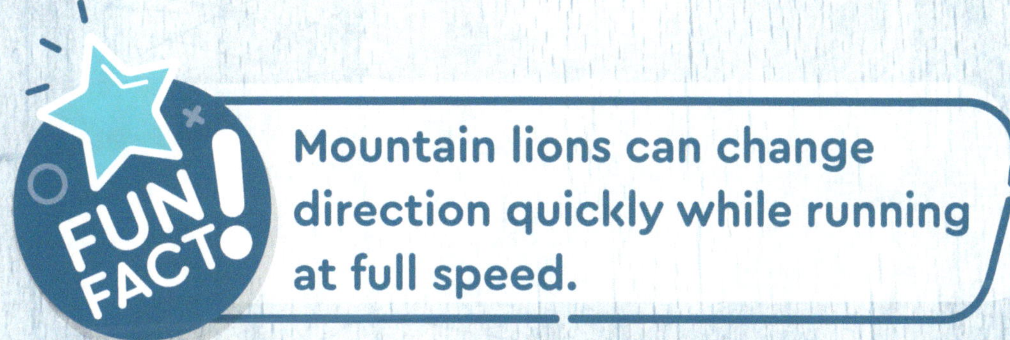

Mountain lions can change direction quickly while running at full speed.

LEAP AND CLIMB

Thump! A mountain lion lands on a high branch. It looks down below.

Mountain lions are great climbers. They use sharp claws to grip tree bark. Strong legs help them jump up steep rocks.

Those strong legs also help them jump very far. One leap can cover 40 feet across flat ground.

Climbing helps them stay hidden. It also helps them watch for prey below. If prey walks under them, they will jump on top to attack.

Mountain lion kittens learn to climb at just two months old. Their mother shows them how.

DAWN
PATROL

Crunch! A mountain lion steps on dry leaves at sunrise.

Mountain lions are most active at dawn and dusk. These times are called twilight hours. The low light helps them stay hidden.

During the day, mountain lions rest to stay cool. They find shady spots under bushes or rocks.

At night, they may hunt or travel. But dawn and dusk are their busiest times. This is when prey animals move around too.

Mountain lions can walk up to 25 miles in one night while moving through their large home area.

LONE
HUNTERS

Screech! A mountain lion calls out. No one answers.

Mountain lions live alone. They do not form packs. Each cat has its own land.

Males have bigger areas than females. A male's land can touch many females' lands. But males stay away from each other.

Mountain lions only meet to mate. Then the male leaves. The mother raises her kittens alone.

Mountain lions mark their territory by scratching trees and leaving scent piles called scrapes.

CALLING CATS

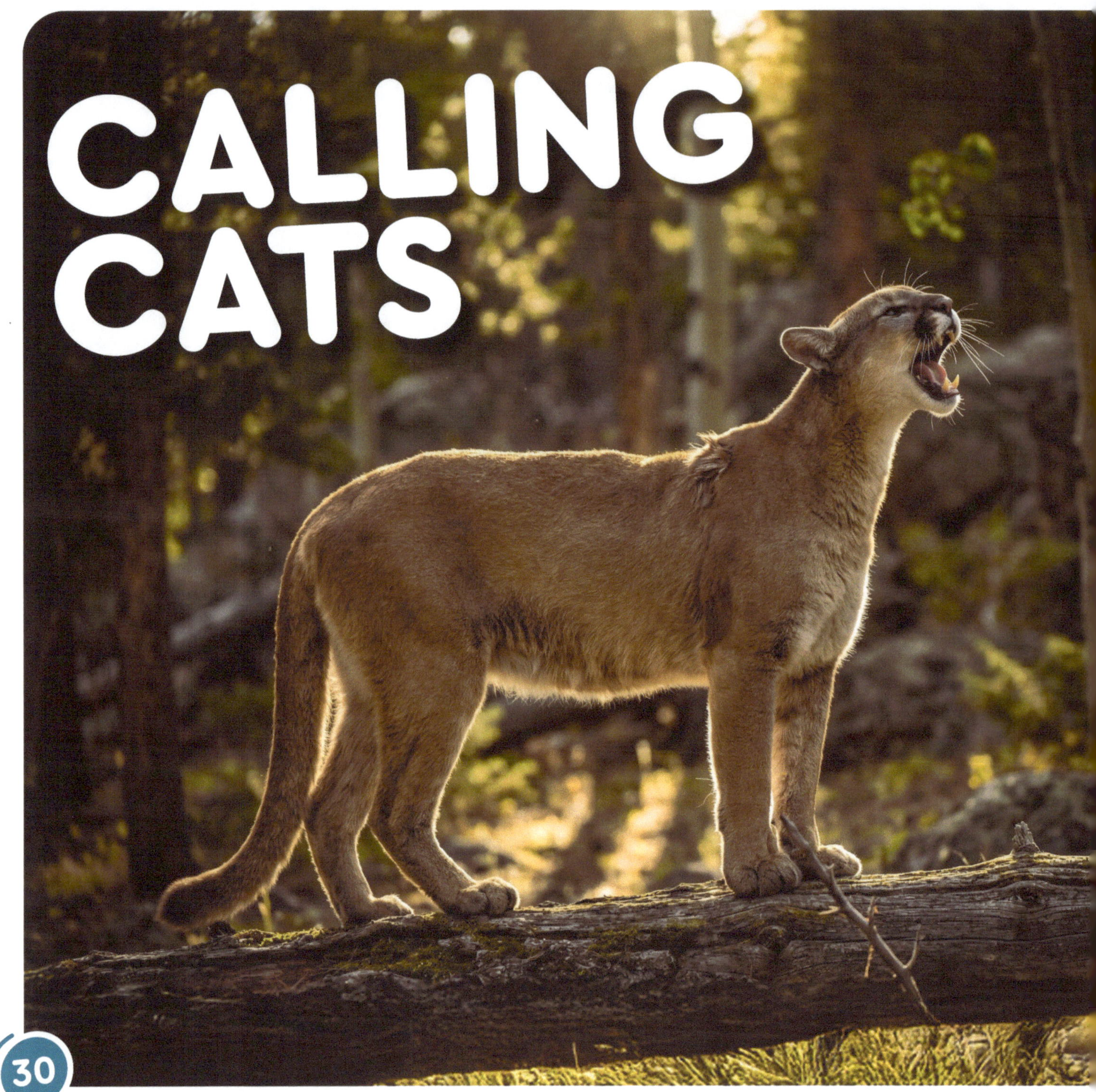

Howl! A female mountain lion calls out at night. She is looking for a mate.

When they are ready to mate females make a special yowling call. Males can hear it from far away.

The sound is loud and eerie. Some people say it sounds like a woman screaming.

Females call for about two weeks. If a male finds her, they stay together for a few days. Then the male leaves to live alone again.

Female mountain lions only spend one to two weeks with a male before living alone again.

CUTE CUBS

DID YOU KNOW?
Mountain lion cubs cannot retract their claws until about three weeks old. This helps them grip their mother.

Squeak! Tiny cubs tumble and play in a hidden den.

Mountain lion cubs are born with spotted fur. The spots help them hide in the brush. These tiny cubs are also born with their eyes closed.

A mother usually has two or three cubs at a time. Newborn cubs weigh about one pound, so they are very small and helpless.

Cubs stay in the **den** for about two months. Their blue eyes open after ten days. As they grow older, their spots slowly fade away.

MOM KNOWS BEST

Grunt! A mother mountain lion carries a cub by its neck.

Mother mountain lions are very protective. They keep their cubs hidden in dens, which might be a cave or thick brush.

Mothers teach cubs how to hunt. They bring meat back to the den for cubs to eat. Cubs watch and learn from their mother.

Cubs stay with their mother for up to two years. She shows them where to find water and how to avoid danger.

When cubs are ready, they leave to find their own territory.

STEALTHY
SURVIVORS

A mountain lion crouches low in the brush.

Mountain lions are survivors. They have lived in the Americas for thousands of years. Many things have changed, but these cats keep going.

When forests are cut down, mountain lions find new homes. They move to different areas. They learn to hunt different prey.

Some mountain lions now live close to cities. They travel through neighborhoods at night. They cross busy roads. They find ways to survive even when people move in.

They live in more places than almost any other wild cat in the world.

LION SPOTTING

Look! A mountain lion moves through tall grass.

Mountain lions are hard to spot. They hide well. They move very quietly. Most people never see one.

Even people who live in mountain lion country rarely see them. These cats are experts at staying hidden. Your best chance to see one up close is at a zoo or wildlife park.

In the wild, look for signs instead. Tracks in mud or snow. Fresh scratch marks on trees. Piles of leaves with a strong smell. But if you find these signs, leave the area. A mountain lion may be nearby.

GLOSSARY

apex predators
Animals at the top that no other animals hunt.

carnivores
Animals that eat only meat.

den
A hidden home where animal babies are born and kept safe.

prey
Animals that are hunted and eaten by other animals

territory
The area where an animal lives and hunts that belongs to it.